# A Cosmiculous Conversation

Copyright © 2017 Dennis Milton Morgan
All rights reserved.
ISBN: 978-0-9893357-4-4

**A GOSPEL INKS PUBLICATION**
www.gospelinks.com

# A Cosmiculous Conversation

Dennis Milton Morgan

# A Cosmiculous Conversation

Published by Gospel Inks
(407)-878-0298
www.gospelinks.com

Cover Design
Lisa Harris-Corbitt
Gospel Inks

Illustrations, where noted, by Waheeda Ramnath
Photography, where noted, by Stephen Fleming
Editing by Monica Morgan and Ashake Patrick

All rights reserved. This book or parts thereof may not be reproduced in any form, stored in a retrieval system or transmitted in any form by any means, electronic, mechanical, photocopy, recording or otherwise, without the written permission of the publisher and author.

ISBN: 978-0-9893357-4-4
Copyright © 2017 by Dennis Milton Morgan

Dennis Milton Morgan's Poetic Collection " A Cosmiculous Conversation" has brought me to appreciate that every human being is definitely programmed by God ( Psalms 100: 1- 3 ). From where did Dennis's thoughts, imagination, words and expressions evolve? I am in utter awe and unimaginable wonder as to how this Poet "CAPTURES"
( What's not there) what nobody can think or see and goes into "CREATIVE MODE" and paints his sights, emotions, thoughts, even illogical themes and unimaginable episodes into something called POETRY. To thoroughly assimilate this man's gift is breath-exhaling, heart pounding and head shaking. I am left in awe and amazement each time I muse thru these Cosmiculous Conversations. Truly Dennis has made me appreciate the God I Serve much more when I think of what God has downloaded in him. I would say that each created man is significant and has a purpose on earth but this man's gift is just as special to me as that of Leonardo da Vinci's or William Shakespeare's. It is wonderful to be a part of his life thru his poetry. May God continue to bless you Dennis... in the name of Jesus.

*Hector Diaz, Designated Pastor*
*Victorious Faith Ministries International/*
*Bishop David Ibeleme*
*Senior Pastor*

For several years Mr. Dennis Morgan has shown an uncanny ability to develop the art of his poetry, growing from meager beginnings, to what he now is -a poet of no mean reckoning. He captivates the reader with his sublime and surreal imaginings, crafted in an absolutely inimitable style. A Cosmiculous Conversation represents an introduction to the kind of mind which, when wrapped around concepts of time, space or being outside of the cosmic realities in which the mundane exists, can massage, knead and weave these concepts, producing a beautiful and glorious conversation unlike that of the ordinary. "The Flair of The Floating Violin" is a particularly masterful piece, and "Behind God's Back" will be well appreciated, especially to persons familiar with the colloquial expression. Mr. Morgan is ever striving to deliver his ultimate poetry – a tapestry of poetic conversation – which peoples of all ages, races, religious persuasions and nationalities can come to appreciate, thus bringing to fruition his ultimate goal of using his very unique talent to add a small but influential voice, to the harmony that is so lacking in this post- modern society."

*Michael Murrell B.Ed*
*Retired Teacher, Educator*
*and Author of "IT's So Simple:*
*An Understandable Computer*
*Learning Experience*

An outpouring of a gifted and bountiful mind that is not limited to ground-level conversations anywhere in the universe. "A Cosmiculous Conversation" is a highly recommended must read documentation so book your flight soon and soar with this poet... it will be a trip you will want to repeat and will never forget.

*Jasmine Swann*
*Retired Teacher / Financial Advisor*
*BA, University of the West Indies*
*French, Spanish, Sociology.*
*MBA (School of Management and Accounting ).*

A Cosmiculous Conversation is a treat for the intellectual and a literary boost for the layman. Dennis Milton Morgan has been able to reveal to this generation important cosmic ideas, ranging from the supreme origins of life to man-made technology that supports it. In prose he has been able to launch readers into wonders of the universe unbridled. After reading this collection of conversations, new perspectives on life and the universe are realized. It would appear that the author of the Cosmos has chosen earthly vessel Morgan to encapsulate his treasures.

*Prisca Jones*
*Dental Hygienist,*
*El Dorado, Trinidad.*

Dennis Morgan's expressions were so well put together that they opened up within me "latent literary experiences". I truly enjoyed reading this book from cover to cover and would highly recommend it to anyone.

*Ms. Carlene Achille*
*Store Manager*

A Cosmiculous Conversation, is truly an example of life's challenges, expectations and disappointments. It inspired me to develop a different way, and possibly a better way of looking at life's experiences. My wish for the author is that he should continue doing this work as it will result in inspiring readers of good literature.

*Delca Joseph*
*Store Supervisor*

# Contents

| | |
|---|---|
| Acknowledgements | 11 |
| Foreword | 14 |
| Dedication | 17 |
| A Cosmiculous Conversation | 20 |
| Free Barabbas | 26 |
| Thank You Jesus | 32 |
| Tell Me Who | 38 |
| God See | 43 |
| A Rosebud In The Morning | 48 |
| Good Morning Moon | 52 |
| Fluorescent Feline | 57 |
| All Because of You | 63 |
| Oh Rustling Wind | 66 |
| Those Unspoken Words | 74 |
| Why Perfection | 79 |
| Floral Cathedral Part 1 | 81 |
| Floral Cathedral Part 2 | 87 |
| A Shady Immortelle | 92 |
| Set On A Hill | 96 |
| Listen To The Night | 100 |
| Behind God's Back | 108 |
| A Shakespearean Refrain | 112 |
| The Flair of the Floating Violin | 118 |

| | |
|---|---|
| A Most Beautiful Day............................ | 135 |
| A Gentle Reminder............................... | 142 |
| It's Already Been Done.......................... | 146 |
| Patmos Rhapsody................................. | 150 |

# Acknowledgements

There is a special group of people that performed what I refer to as "angelic tasks", by nudging me towards this book. I acknowledge their strategic importance to the development of this conversation.

First there was Noel Farrell, who literally reminded me of my history to convince me that I had the tools to do poetry when he wanted a co-author/per-former to work with. God used that boy to change my life... thank you, Noel.

Then there was Dereck Jones. Dereck is the only person I have met that has a mental picture of my poetic potential that compares with the one I have in my mind. Dereck sees things that few people know exist.

Then there is Sarah Beckett, an artist with a glittering brush that can capture sensitive words, along with the jazz music band of Michael (Mikey) Germaine. Sarah and Mikey showed me that my poetry could speak in unison with other genres and deliver an unforgettable entertainment experience.

Then there is Harvey Burris, the first person that spotted the potency in my poetry.

Then there were connoisseurs Alexander Holder and Barbara Brown who thought they heard something that was different enough to pull me aside and talk to me seriously.

And then, those spas, who are celebrants conversant in cerebral rudiments, especially Edwin "Stretch" Gooding , Glen Dookie ,  Conrad " Job" Francis, Winston "Alberto" Albert,  the Bordes of Galba, Keith "Prezo " Joseph, the "Hebrews from the hill" , my soul brothers of " Love City ", the word-trekking youths of that era from Diamond Vale  and all those other batters who I threw curved balls and doosras at and they were skilful enough to hit them out the park. I thank you and I acknowledge the positive impact you had in my life.

Then there are my very special poetry spas; people that I use as critics and a source of fuel when I am entering new zones of poetry. These folks like Bro. Benny and the inspirational "Church of God" congregation that I was truly blessed to worship with; Winston Timothy, Tony Peters, Gemma Ramelize, Corey Joseph, Maria Cruickshank-Gibbs, Olderson Josiah and his immeasurable ministry of "poetry for the youths", and many others who appear to be pre-occupied but when you get to know them they turn out to be poetry buffs to the core.

Finally, my wife Pat and daughter Abi, Siblings and congregations I fellowship with provide a consistent reservoir of spiritual supply from which I could draw and be constantly replenished with God's word. I thank you all.

*Dennis Milton Morgan*
**POET**

# Foreword

From beneath the chorus of shouts and obscene gestures popularly used as the medium of communication among the many agitated people of the planet, this poet has a burden on his heart for a civilization, obviously suffering from conversation dysfunction; you don't have to listen hard to detect that the human spirit is starving for inspiration. How do we understand each other? How do we get anything done? Today, we live in a world of gridlock driven by restricted partisan perspective.

You know... I do believe that God's creative juices were activated by His desire for mutual conversation. The Bible says that in the cool of the evening He came into the garden to talk with man because He knew that relationship is maintained for better or worse by the quality of communication you sustain. Then as man veered off into his treacherous pathway, God prophesied that in the last days there will be wars and rumors of wars and to counter-act the communication deficiencies of our time; one of the tools he put in place for mankind is inspirational poetry.

While this poet is not suggesting that inspirational poetry is the panacea that solves the full spectrum of human disagreements, from petty crime to military disputes, I do believe that inspirational poetry provides a quantum leap towards restoring civility to our planet. It's a big challenge and we need your help; the preachers and positive motivators cannot do it on their own. The planet needs all hands on deck. Way beyond a song in time with chime a good poem can be a sermonette with rhyme. Together we can take the wobble out of the planet.

The Apostle Paul was sufficiently concerned about the craft of communication to admonish in Colossians 4:6 to "Let your speech be always with grace, seasoned with salt, that you may know how to answer every man." I was also impressed with what I refer to as Pope Benedict's, non-denominational, essay to the World Communication Day forum in 2012 which highlighted a balance between speaking and silence, which to me ought to set us apart in creation. Among other things he proceeded to say, "By remaining silent, we allow the other person to speak; to express him or herself and avoid being tied simply to our own words and ideas without them being adequately tested." Think about it, an exchange of ideas is how you can use speech to develop the muscles of your mind.

So, I invite you to relax, where ever or whenever you can, pick up the book and fly on the wings of its poetic word strings to places and emotions other genres struggle to reach. I hope you enjoy this collection of poems as much as I enjoyed writing them, just for you. Then, after re-harnessing and re-distributing the potential of your passion, I hope you will join this campaign to make communication......something to savor, again.

The planet and its people need you more than ever. There is no argument to it... just poetry.
Thank you, very much. Thank you, very kindly.

*Dennis Milton Morgan*
**POET**

# Dedication

*Dedicated To The Wider Community*

Indeed, my poetry is the sum total of my life... my scenic passage through time. So, to the community that fashioned my life and made me what I am today, I thank you and I dedicate this book to you.

To my wife Pat and daughter Abi... you provided the human and spiritual infrastructure needed for a man to launch out into destiny. Talking about infrastructure... thank you Debbie Sookoo for your timely, strategic interventions that cannot be evaluated. I hope this work will inspire you all to ace God's purpose for your lives.

I dedicate this work to all my siblings who showed me that excellence was within reach....... and especially George Morgan who assumed responsibility in my life that God earmarked for a father.

To my peers in Morvant and Diamond Vale ( where my adult writing sprouted ), my school mates that I interacted with while attending Morvant Anglican School, Queen's Royal College, Caribbean Union College and Seneca College in Toronto; in those institutions I was exposed to excellence that I am still trying to measure and fully savour. I remember those mates and teachers vividly and I dedicate this book to all of you and the classical times we had in the sixties and early seventies in Trinidad... it was a bit turbulent but at the same time, it was the best in existence.

I dedicate this book to those I have casually met and thought that they were latent writers and needed a little nudge, and they responded and are now budding poets. I hope you "Stay the Course".

To my deceased mom, Leotha Morgan, I dedicate this book in appreciation of the spiritual environment she provided for my development. To my daughter Abi , my nieces and nephews and all young folks coming up to do greater things than their predecessors........especially Carolyne and Andrea Morgan and Pastor Roger Wade who have all plugged into the word in a spectacular way, I dedicate this book to you.

Finally... to my publisher Lisa Harris- Corbitt, and manager Dereck Jones, I say thanks for everything, and

I dedicate this book to our professional development. " Stay the Course... all the way."

*Dennis Milton Morgan*
**POET**

## A Cosmiculous Conversation

*Prepaid and precious... Miraculous! Cosmiculous!!!*
*We could have those conversations everyday*
*yet peculiar and presumptuous...*
*we seldom allow him to have his say*
*his wisdom seldom comes into play,*
*at best and in our favor we deliver... one way.*
*Reluctantly, we get off pace to allocate space*
*and with eyes that cannot absorb*
*the brilliance emanating from his face*
*we seldom credit his grace to embrace the choice*
*to use our inner ear*
*to capture the words reverberating off the chords modulating*
*the musical tones of his heavenly voice.*

*My friends... conversation was centrifugal*
*to the Tower of Babel*
*'twas from man's intensive horizontal*
*vocal inter-connectivity came ideas*
*implemented utilizing primitive procedures...*

Illustration by Waheeda Ramnath

*to straddle stratospheres, to breach the vicinity  
of that gleaming golden city  
strutting beyond the boundaries  
of those sensitive, holy heavenlies.  
So God, confounded their speech  
so the benefits of vertical conversations he could teach,  
as co-creators mankind's need to studiously listen  
to profound signals, like sand on a beach,  
in the cool of the evening…  
when the alpha and omega is oozing outreach.*

*Indeed… conversation is a blessing from God  
yet we live by the sword.  
Full of words… we curse and widely misuse, mankind  
and even God, we abuse.  
Its power we don't comprehend…  
its pitfalls and sharp edges we perpetuate  
again and again, conversations with God  
have its prime of place…  
its potency and poetry is daily going to waste.*

*My Savior, and most importantly, My Lord…*
*I hear you loud and clear*
*you conquered death and despise fear,*
*you unravel time…. unforgiveness you see as a crime,*
*when you talk planets unfurl*
*and without end you unleashed our world.*

*Conversation with God… my mind takes a leap*
*it transforms a dwarf confined in a perilous trough,*
*uncharted and deep*
*into a mountainous giant of a peek, unsurmounted and steep.*

*Conversations with God… a poet strives to discern*
*its syntax and meanings, phonetics and gleanings.*

*And as we learn I will forever yearn,*
*for not just a two but a three-way with you*
*including my talkative, narrative compulsive,*
*noisy and continuously speech*
*combative brother and sister,*

*to fashion and turn by turn… to churn.*

"*Oh Heavenly Father, I copy… I know I've been sloppy
but now… now… it's over to you!*"
*And with eardrums well dusted,
your servant comes well trusted,
and with ear lodes big like those of an elephant or even a cow,
I… I humbly, humbly bow and I'll tell you this,
therein lies the thesis
of a cosmiculous never ambiguous,
universe crisis saving, conversation…
and remember to mix your talking
with a good helping of profound listening
and much more than a semblance
of pre-utterance inspired thinking… and of course to elevate
the discourse, give voluntary yet spiritually mandatory
honor to the hierarchy now present in your verbal sanctuary
with heavenly cheers of spontaneous halleluiahs
concluding with an ascending
cosmiculous never frivolous, amen ending.*

*And to you out there...communicating without care*

*while arrogantly straddling the stratosphere...*

*those precious cosmiculous conversations are harmonious*

*inter-actions emanating from excursions into biblical truths,*

*creation observations and a lifestyle of prayer*

*assisted by a sensitive ear,*

*because it may be in rolling thunder*

*or in a gentle whisper, but God's voice is always near*

*and it will make your life glisten,*

*so, go ahead and talk, then hush, don't rush;*

*while you studiously listen*

*to that till, soft voice... it is your heaven given choice.*


*Finally, permit me to say, that earth crisis overcomers,*

*negotiators, Good Samaritan care-givers*

*and all heaven bound sojourners, talk that way.*

# Free Barabbas

"Free Barabbas!" was the cry of the crowd at the full stretch

of their lungs they were shouting aloud

"Free Barabbas!" but my savior stood still...

cause he knew their emotions

visualized and felt the pain from his lacerations...

oozing with the blood he was destined to spill

along this God chosen Via Dolorosa pathway he must follow

to fulfill... all rugged and a-winding

with man's Redemption a– beckoning... all bruised and

cross-laden he had to go a-trekking

Step by step he could see himself climbing

with obedience and goodwill,

ascending with his altar towards an excruciating death

that was awaiting at the top of that dirgeful hill.

Meanwhile, their professed righteousness

made them more merciless...

*and with another uncompromising shrill*
*they moved in for the kill...*
*"Barabbas! Free Barabbas!!!"*

*But Barabbas at least to the Roman Emperor*
*was a predictable repeat offender*
*at best and at worst a Barbarous murderer,*
*a Jewish warrior, a Roman Destroyer*
*spreading terror at the Devil's behest.*

*"Free Barabbas!!!"*
*The crowd proclaimed again...*
*but the lamb stood stoic and almost impartial*
*as he prepared to be slain.*

*"Free Barabbas!!!"*
*Echoed off the stones etched with the opulence*
*that plastered Pilate's hall*
*"Crucify Him!!!" Was their response to Pilate's plea*
*about his innocence and totally misguided fall.*

"Free Barabbas and Crucify this Jesus!!!"
The crowd crescendoed in anger,
"For he is worse than a murderer…
this blaspheming liar, claims he is a God and a King
and has now gone and committed the one unforgiveable sin."

But, maybe, although and even until…
preceded mocking questions Pilate and Herod raised
as they used puny estimates to limit the powers
of this celestial crusader…
who stealthily launched profound answers
whispered from the background of a battered
yet blissfully confident gaze.

"Free Barabbas!!!" the crowd demanded,
"and Crucify this Jesus in the worse way
and to the highest degree, and remember
to show no mercy and remember to prolong the agony…"
it commanded.

Illustration by Waheeda Ramnath

*So Pilate with grace...*

*reached for his towel and water*

*so he could free himself thru time and space*

*from the responsibility of being a willing partner,*

*but when he looked and read between the lines*

*embossed on the perpetrator's face*

*he got a glimpse of his resolve to endure*

*the contents of the cross this dreamer was sent to embrace.*

*Pilate washed his hands and swirled his gown...*

*turned his back to the throng*

*and then he began to ponder about the threat*

*and from whom it was greater.*

*Pilate wrapped his mind around the dilemma*

*of having to free a killer*

*and crucify a crusader gone wrong.*

*Pilate was reluctant... Barabbas was nonchalant*

*and Satan in hell was expectant*

*and they were all trapped*

*but the saints in heaven clapped...*

*oh yes, the saints in heaven clapped*

*because they knew that the lamb that was sent*

*to lay down his life and was compliant*

*would on the third day be raised again*

*as a lion... triumphant.*

*Yes the saints in heaven clapped because they knew*

*that one day people like me and you*

*would come to understand the value embedded*

*in the victory won on that day*

*when they freed Barabbas...*

*For Alas, 'twas a chance at freedom for all of us...*

*Thank you, Jesus.*

## Thank You Jesus

*Still he persisted… even before succumbing*
*to that mandatory death*
*played out on that transitory set*
*erected on that dirgeful hill…*
*still, he delivered goodwill*
*when he petitioned his heavenly father*
*to have mercy on Pilate, the Roman soldier,*
*even the Sanhedrin and also the throng…*
*then he hung his head down*
*and when he was ready his life to relinquish*
*he whispered, "it is finished."*

*'Twas after praying for forgiveness…*
*for they know not what they do*
*and just before his father shook the very earth*
*so he could rend the veil in two.*

*Oh yeah… he was up there where the air was rare…*

*hanging from his wooden pulpit,*

*our sinless remit reached his human mission summit*

*when, although, barely audible,*

*whenever I read my Bible… I must admit*

*I hear syllable after echoing syllable, submit…*

*"into your hands I commit my spirit."*

*And I believe the saints and angels*

*gave a standing ovation*

*while beholding scenes that were fashioned*

*before the foundation of creation*

*and on the occasion of the crucifixion…*

*the angelic host praised him the most*

*and were especially pleased that morning,*

*when he delivered those dangling keys*

*when the earth's new dispensation*

*was officially launched*

*and emphatically christened.*

**What a Cosmiculous Victory!**
**Our Savior's "Empty Tomb" Is His Commitment To Our Eternity.**

*Oh yes… 'twas a miraculous resurrection;*

*for he was risen*

*with countenance that glowed,*

*feet and palm wounds that flowed*

*and earthly apparel that glistened.*

*And from across the floor I saw angels stood in awe*

*when mankind's praises soared*

*and eventually came ashore,*

*they folded their wings and attentively listened.*

*And you may not believe the harmony*

*when they sang a celestial melody*

*that crescendoed into chorus*

*as my thoughts, momentarily and ponderingly curious,*

*reverted to callous Barabbas*

*and the role he played*

*that was not just miscellaneous.*


*And I saw stunned disciples skywardly gazing*

*at their savior waving while disappearing*

*into a heaven-bound cloud*

*beaming at a possessive, reflective crowd*

*singing his praises aloud.*


*While... ringside and in the mix*

*his disciples stood transfixed*

*with roaming memories salvaging strategies*

*from intricate passages of his eternal messages*

*with which for souls we must all go fishing.*

*But now… on this trembling perch*
*before building his church*
*emotions within them lurch*
*as together, they watched him*
*slowly ascending without fuss*
*from out of the planet's swirling, crystallized dust.*

*And I can still see angels that were previously escorting,*
*now re-assuring that … "that same Jesus*
*will one day return*
*to duly immortalize us.*
*And, oh yes, in that ultimate process,*
*all knees will bow and all tongues confess."*
*And in unison and with good reason,*
*they all began to sing*
*while in the background*
*I heard the soothing sound of the harp*
*intermingling with flings*
*of scintillating violin strings…*
*and bells rang as they sang*

*in that stupendous cosmic setting*

*"Thank You, loving Jesus...*
*for you are indeed Lord of Lords*
*and indeed King of Kings."*

## Tell Me Who

Who causes a warm windless plight to gust,
cooling a stagnant moon lit evening,
and turbulent seas to rush when fishes below are sleeping
or nonchalantly relaxing.

Tell me who… Amazing yet, reluctantly revealing.

Who revs the earth to spin around the sun
to fetch a morning,
Who paints the skies in hues using angles
dipping with visual effects lavishly dripping.
Amazing and kaleidoscoping.

Who snaps the twig from the branch
laden with dew or snow or from a careless bird
gazing and chirping while landing.

**Aurora Borealis**

*Who conducts withered leaves waffling downwards*
*when their music-filled, chlorophyll lives*
*are no longer absorbing, replenishing or rustling.*
*Amazing… all members naturally syncopating.*


*Who embroiders a rainbow with silver lining…*
*to highlight a covenant he is keeping,*
*and litters snow-capped mountains with confetti that glitters*
*when the crazy twists of the Aurora Borealis light rays*
*in the northern skies go blissfully dancing.*
*Those phenomena are celestially entertaining.*


*Who prescribed freedom for the woman?*
*unworthy, blood-thirsty men*
*found guilty of committing adultery.*


*Who mustered strength to petition his father passionately*
*so his crucifiers could receive mercy.*
*Tell me who…*
*not just Amazing but benevolently all embracing.*

*Who foretells days unlived complete with drama unwritten,*
*knows the glory of orbits unspun and rewards generations*
*with good deeds unsmitten.*
*And just for fun, he can unfurl the beauty*
*of an unblossomed flower exponentially into a…*
*heavenly wonder and is accurate with the intensity*
*he calibrates for even an unflung sun.*

*Tell me who?? Who?? Who to pursue…*
*there is no comparative response from you*
*Yet death, despair and paralyzing fear*
*are main components in the residue of this earth issue.*

*Tell me who….*
*A loving, living God of the Holy Trinity… that's who,*
*that's true*
*with this planet just a small clue of his all-powerful*
*ever expanding purview,*
*Tell me who??*
*I'm just teasing to activate inspired thinking*

*when vacillating.*

*Cause you may not know The How or When…*
*beware of your human trend and earthly blend*
*but deep in your heart right from the very start,*
*I know you know The Why and most definitely…*
*I know you know The Who.*

## God See

*Many have tried but none can refute*
*that pictures don't lie*
*and mirrors reflect the whole truth*
*and those satellite surveillance skyware*
*that orbit the outer stratosphere*
*record transactions at the ground level*
*as we do our earthly commute,*

*And then... when we go into the realms*
*of the third heaven, over yonder*
*in the area put asunder*
*from the plunder of the human blunder,*
*up there in what must be the observatory rotunda*
*recoils the spirit that created*
*and can effortlessly scan the universe*
*winkless and boundless its capacity to traverse, reverse*
*and among all other things converse*

*and this poet thinks it's a curse to clandestinely disperse*
*the seeds of your deeds*
*hoping that this omnipotent, omniscient spirit*
*will not identify those fruits and from his purse*
*accordingly reimbursed.*

*My friends.... the blessing of this creation commerce affords*
*the luxury for me to say emphatically*
*That whatever we do now and into the future*
*will be subjected to "data capture"*
*Including the things of the past*
*brought forward from our history will be processed well,*
*randomly and or sequentially in the virtual, eternal reality*
*of heaven or hell, will someone pray tell*

*the terse of this verse is that poetic justice*
*is immersed in the things we do*
*that undoubtedly, God See.*
*God See the wheat and tares fight for space*
*as they grow together,*

*he sees the unjust enjoy sunshine*
*while deserving devastating stormy weather,*


*he sees shortcuts taken towards gain*
*feels the pain when the innocent is slain*
*is repulsed by the stain of sin*
*encroaching with its darkness*
*in contrast to the righteousness offered to man*
*after subduing the death of Calvary*
*with the victory of life and light served on a platter for man*
*over Lucifer to win, reversing the spin of sin.*


*Believe you me, my friends…*
*from the foundation God knew*
*and God see.*


*God See the things you do and your payment is due,*
*he will even compensate on the things you meditate*
*and in the lonely nightmare you dare*
*he will secure the area if his presence you share*

*but his hands are tied when his justice is tried*
*although with repentance you see*
*the brilliance in the grace of his mercy...*

*because it's from the purity and intentions of the heart*
*is where your actions all start*
*and from where God calibrates then calculates*
*so as to separate the guilty from the innocent part.*

*It's no folly... you must let your soul be the beneficiary*
*of the things God See.*

*Oh yes, my brother and sister...*
*with eyes keener than an eagle*
*and with homing systems deadlier than a shark*
*the things you do in the dark*
*are magnified and duly classified, it's no stroll in the park...*
*God See, so don't skylark*
*in this universe your life is naked and stark*
*and useless silencing the witness*

*or even the dogs that bark... you keep missing the mark.*

*For God's payment is many times more potent*
*than those received from the human element*
*this earth is a test so don't settle for less...*
*beware God's redress.*

*My friend... from the foundation to an eternity without end,*
*God See... most definitely.*

# A Rosebud In The Morning

I stumbled across God...

as he created a new beginning

'Twas on the cusp of a golden and "oh...

what a beautiful dawning

Inadvertently, I had opened the door

and he was right there... but was well aware,

And he just smiled and waved me to come see...

This sight soaked in the encroaching morning light

Just beyond the shade of the canopy

that covered the steps to my front balcony

And as I moved in closer I could hear him whisper

"for sure...

I know, you will take good care of this flower,"

He then took his time to complete his final touches... then he handed me this...

*This rosebud, released from the grips of his tender clutches.*

*And as he spoke.... the wind broke*
*into a most musical whistle*
*As he highlighted the functions of its thorns*
*And warned of the dangers that lurk*
*Amongst the weeds and the thick thistle*

*And he said "my friend,*

*on you… all heaven depend,*

*So I have decided to you this morning…*

*my words I will lend."*


*He said, "please prune and nurture and*

*Do the daily watering and overall parenting…*

*Fertilize your stewardship*

*with the nutrients of a wholesome*

*And above all a holy relationship…*

*And before long time will reveal*

*a pearl as the petals of this flower unfurl*

*From the best rosebuds that ever blossomed*

*in this whole wide world…*


*And you can take comfort*

*for I will multiply your human effort*

*When I add my supernatural leaven*

*To the potential of these rosebuds …*

*that I personally transplanted from my garden*

*Just beyond my balcony brought here to earth
using special transability
To convey the excellence and unique beauty
Of a rosebud creation using celestial propagation,
an idea sanctioned in heaven."*

*"so my friend……
in your hands you hold an awesome responsibility
So please take good care of this rosebud…
especially in the dawning of its morning for me …
and there is no mistaking…
You make me smile when I see you
enjoying landscaping…
for there is no other earthly activity that more accurately
confirms an angelic connectivity.*

*Thank you very much…
and thank you very kindly.*

## Good Morning Moon

Good morning moon… I see you stayed around

to remind this town

Of the splendour you possess,

For when you orbit high

And wonder wearily towards the west…

you escape the night sky

To inspire startled man

with the brilliance you have been blest,


And with authority supreme

You spike the morning with the well

buffed glitter of your gleam

According to the words the creator gave

You kept darkness in check with the light you reflect

So even mortal man asleep in a cave

Awaiting another glimpse of your majestic moonlight

That not even a dark night

or a total eclipse could enslave

In the clutches of a glow less enclave

*But good morning moon ... your light fades all too soon*
*As you compete with the boss of the day*
*To our village you belong after dancing all night*
*to the moods of an unmodulated song*

*That's why in the morning*
*your light will still hold sway*

*I remember your waltz*
*and how you expose steps that are false*
*The spins and the swirls in gear that you reveal*
*The wink in your eye as you crisscross the sky*
*The whispers from your craters*
*that you cannot conceal*

*And good morning moon...*
*you eat my heart with your gold spoon*
*I have never seen a celestial event quite like this*
*With night transformed into dawn, yet... a moonbeam*
*lingers on my lawn*

*As the business of the day marches on with a twist*

*As I witness the bliss of love*

*among heavenly bodies persist*

*To see the earth and its moon …*

*swish, with light hearted fun around the sun*

*Is the joy of which this universe consists*

*And I cherish the ecstasy emanating from the embrace*

*of this early morning kiss*

*And good morning moon…*

*your high tide floats my lagoon*

*And all nature swoon at the visual crescendos*

*that make up your tune*

*Securely fettered with clearly no strings attached*

*Bombarding asteroids and meteoroids*

*I see you snatch and stash in your hatch*

*There is no union in the universe to surpass*

*this celestial catch,*

*And as I gaze at your florescent gleam*
*In the foreground of this golden early morning beam*
*My heart leaps very steep*
*When I consider the things you illuminate*
*when you procrastinate*
*And the things you keep at bay*
*as we waltz on our way*
*Towards the dawning of this…this majestic morning*
*As you go unfolding the petals of this beautiful flower*
*Blooming and adorning the thresholding*
*of yet another heavenly day.*

*And so… good morning moon,*
*whether September, January or June*
*I will shout across the lagoon… majestic moon*
*Your light fades all too soon.*

# Fluorescent Feline

"Fluorescent Feline...
Wait Nuh Girl, you got eyes that...
glow in the night,
those given in heavenly matrimony to reflect true love...
unrequited.

Oh... Fluorescent Beauty, silent and sublime in sight
You are my Fluorescent Sweetie...
Planet Earth's one and only orbiting satellite."

"And with grace and precision in rhythm...
we waltz the night away,
under a pure filtered light as if ejected from circumcision,
you inadvertently lengthen my day,
you customize loving feelings
as you enchant the planet with play

**Photography by Stephen Fleming**

*but most of all… you entice a weary world  
to behold the splendour of the Milky Way."*

*"And just after a sundip unleashes  
the ferocity of its story,  
you….. my fluorescent feline respond  
by switching on your superlative glory.*

*I watch as you rev into a unique position  
and when in close proximity  
I admire your definition…  
and when full and just about spilling over,  
you nestle right next to me…  
just like a sensuous lover.*

*Oh Fluorescent Feline, come hang over my valley,  
come warm my heart  
And let me drink directly  
from your curvaceous body."*

*But there are times when things get steamy*
*and cycles intercept*
*When instincts become wayward*
*and darkness eclipse your drunken step*
*Though fleeting it is a reminder*
*that light and love are special gifts*
*Wrapped by the hands of God…*
*and should not be seen as a mere given*
*But as enforced from the tip of his sword*

*Yes, light and love are exciting tools of creation*
*generated from deep inner and outer space*
*With love reflecting the intensity of God's compassion*
*and it ain't no joke,*
*your sun-soaked fluorescent glow… you know,*
*Is symbolic of the brilliance emanating from his face."*

*"Fluorescent Feline, planetary pleasures*
*your whim and fancy be;*
*And just like a gateman… you signal time slots*

*and tide spots out and in,*

*to and fro can't miss your glow*

*as you orchestrate dynamics and frequency*

*and intentionally disperse periodic monotony…*

*I'm in a magnetic ecstasy."*


"Fluorescent Feline, please tell me your name…

but hold your tongue (shhhh)

and don't bother I will love you all over just the same.


Fluorescent Feline…

remember on earth it is a cert

that I will always swoon

for your dazzling Fluorescent Moon…

and remember that I will always love you alone, forever."


"Fluorescent Feline… even though you sometimes retreat behind a dark timeline and I can't see you, your beauty remains foremost somewhere in the foreground of this…

this light sensitive shrine."

*"Fluorescent Feline...*

*you enlighten and energize the remote sinews*

*Of my captivated planetic, poetic, romantic mind*

*and although I must share your beauty*

*with the rest of the universe...*

*A beauty that grows*

*like the bouquet of ...*

*a connoisseur's wine*

*I'm blest because this life is excellent...*

*cause you are my resplendent,*

*almost translucent, fluorescent feline,*

*Ummh... I'm so glad you're MINE."*

## All Because Of You

*when stars were made to blaze unglazed*

*the mould God used, meh lady... was you.*

*to shine un-timed, true love on earth to find...*

*and it's all because of you.*


*'twas far more potent than the words God used*

*in creation and with artwork that is plain to see,*

*God created woman as the embodiment*

*of a celestial revelation,*

*the manifestation of an optical exhilarating exclamation ...*

*of the blissful joy his heaven could be.*


*yes... God came down to earth*

*to create for a moment,*

*to ignite nerves and carve curves...*

*with classical intent.*


*he used his very hands, and believe you me,*

*it had to be a he, and oh yes,*

*he took the ultimate artistic responsibility*
*to weave the fibres of what we enjoy today*
*in this multi-functional female entity.*

*meh lady love, it's all because of you…*
*it's all because of you.*
*God surpassed the splendour of the universe*
*when he formed and rightly fashioned*
*then duly commissioned the reality of you.*

*it's all because of you… it's all because of you.*
*God knew he had to discontinue*
*man's emotional starvation…*
*his sensual signal stagnation*
*and most of all his intimacy alienation.*

*he knew he had to fill the shoe to deliver*
*the queen of creation*
*complete with a quest to pursue…*
*an event which was not just strategic nor poetic*

*but in my mind it was totally epic*

*and indeed cosmically due.*

*meh lady love… it was all because of you.*

## Oh Rustling Wind

"Oh rustling wind, whenever you are around

I notice… you no ordinary breeze,

for when my soul is tired and restless …

you chase my cares

from the deep recesses of my thought processes

and with a gentle sneeze… if you please,

you send them scurrying out the dark corridors

of my mind exits

and then… you put my spirit at ease,


and especially on moonless nights

when shadows playfully hide

the unharnessed rays of our scorching sun…

you cool down my days

and knowingly set my sails

to spectacular horizons

after putting my anxieties on the run…

oh rustling wind."

"I've heard great renditions
from award winning orchestras
all resplendent and replete
with Trini G-pans and Stradivarius violins
played by doctor rated musicians
under the command of baton waving conductors
who are accomplished grand-masters
and young virtuosos standing tall on pedestals
adorned with score sheets and tuxedos... complete,

but... no man-made symphony can compare
with your harmonic quality that grace my ear
and can duplicate your instrumentation
when strummed or blown
as with the musical message you effortlessly convey
as if directly from the heavenly father's throne...
oh rustling wind."

"I do declare... we ought to not just appreciate
but savour the rapture of your tonal texture

*and the soothing effects of your therapeutic sounds,*
*as you caressingly provide us with filtered air*
*in this dimension where*
*God's breath of life so freely abounds...*

*oh rustling wind."*
*"You bring a mood that lovers and haters alike...*
*involuntarily adore.*

*You are the main ingredient*
*when mixing a heavenly ambience,*
*the kind that all nature, uncontrollably crave for.*

*I can't help but notice the birds and the bees*
*and even hyenas become stirred*
*with their protruding antennas aroused,*
*and after scanning frequencies*
*they respond to your breeze*
*with a spontaneous ramajay, if you may,*
*about the signals they heard*

streaming thru the leaves of these strategic trees...
with a rustling that you so resoundingly
but yet, so subtly espouse...
oh rustling wind."


"But suddenly... nature can break into a quarrel
and gentle swirls can change into a gust
and the fury of hurricanes, blizzards, cyclones and tornadoes
can come a-searching,
like an angry elephant... a-swinging its heavy tusk
and these musical leaves can be stripped off
as trees are up-rooted


lives can be displaced as river mouths are silted
and this breeze... that was once a-rustling
can be modified into a monster
coming at you a-howling,
as it modulates a different melody
from a God left with no other remedy
like when he had to destroy

*Sodom and Gomorra's territory*
*and when he gave Noah the specifications*
*to build a big ferry*
*that would float off an in-land,*
*and oh yes... water-less jetty.*

*But if you tune in very carefully... like the animals,*
*you will pick up those signals very clearly*
*in the rhythms of the rustling wind."*

*"So, my friends... when next you hear a breeze*
*that makes you want to listen*
*it might just be God making an appearance*
*in the form of an abstract person,*
*not like when he personally visited Adam and Eve*
*in the cool of the Garden*
*and brought along this mellow breeze that cause still leaves*
*to be slightly shaken,*
*I can almost hear his audible voice*
*saying to all relevant elements*

*and with a reassuring grin…*
*oh rustling wind, oh rustling wind,*
*come share a bit of heaven's joy with my next of kin."*

*"Oh yes, my friends… there are noises that you hear*
*and then there those that soothe the soul,*
*there are feelings that nestle up to you*
*that's worth much more than silver and gold,*
*there are words that are spoken and released*
*in the air and with flair*
*God used a few potent words to create this…*
*this universe*
*but, yet with man… he longs to converse.*

*And so… as we go on this spin,*
*comforted by the rustling wind*
*I'd like to know the source*
*from where your gentle breezes blow*
*and how you quench my senses tonight???*
*As moons and stars and other heavenly elements*

*align themselves in my imaginary line of sight,*
*I behold as they bow in unison*
*at our creator's awesome might*
*including the rustling wind ... this rustling wind,*

*You soothe the rough edges of my spiritual plight,*
*Oh, rustling wind... this rustling wind*
*You smooth the rough air pockets*
*of my earthly flight*
*Oh, rustling wind... tonight*

*You are my spectacular zephyr, my Atlantic*
*on and off shore lover*
*And you take me to places unknown...*
*unstrummed... and unblown*
*Where to understand my mind, just cannot begin,*
*Oh rustling wind... this rustling wind...*
*oh rustling... wind."*

## Those Unspoken Words

*I thought I heard something… just an inkling*
*A resounding string of words that just were not said*
*It quickly became an exclamation… sounded like shouting*
*Going round the chambers in my head.*

*It peeled with emotion, reverberated with passion,*
*Crescendoed with full participation…*
*I could hear it loud and clear*
*Pounding out signals… Profound, not vague or dismal*
*But rhythmic…. against the drums in my ear.*

*It's language universal and intent celestial*
*It beamed with a glow and a flow*
*It never tried to confuse, bemuse or abuse*
*It amazed and amused me instead.*

BLAH
BLAH
BLAH
BLAH
BLAH
BLAH
BLAH
BLAH
BLAH
BLAH
BLAH
BLAH
BLAH
BLAH
BLAH
BLAH
BLAH
BLAH
BLAH
BLAH
BLAH
BLAH
BLAH
BLAH
BLAH
BLAH
BLAH
BLAH
BLAH
BLAH
BLAH
BLAH
BLAH
BLAH
BLAH
BLAH
BLAH
BLAH
BLAH
BLAH
BLAH
BLAH

*I stopped and I listened*

*as the message sparkled and glistened*

*It flared and enveloped life lush*

*and with a dynamic hush… that gave me a joy within*

*it made me calculate that*

*a deluge of un-edited words can truncate*

*and true feelings can be de-railed in phonetic spin.*


*So when next thoughts are composed*

*let feeble words respectfully recede and repose*

*Next to where you will know the score*

*For when your thoughts beckon*

*you must let your instincts strengthen*

*And your spiritual inspiration will hopefully open the door.*


*To an ocean of language… not just verbiage*

*Silently modulating beyond a noisy shore*

*from where potential stutter to deliver*

*And unfulfilled purpose clamour for more*

*While shifting thru an obscene heap of toxic literary garbage... I must confide I lied*
*But I did discern those unspoken words*
*yearned to be quickly salvaged.*


*So my musical girl and musical fellow...*
*"don't let thoughtless words run the show,*
*they create an empty, noisy, bitter chorale to swallow,'*
*and coronate you "king of the shallow."*
*But this life is complete and could be sweet*
*When below the surface you go... where still waters run deep*
*And is replete with treasures that hurl,*
*swirls of beautifully crafted*
*spoken and unspoken pearls to poetically express it.*


*So let's keep the door ajar by raising the communication bar*
*and keep catapulting yourself over the summit*
*even over a brazen, well spoken...*
*distant but not totally silent*
*BLAZING STAR... can't you feel it!!! I'm sure you can.*

*Because its Solar Rays compel you to listen*
*In a world where transmission is sometimes totally broken*
*but those notes from glittering melodies*
*are no worthless token*
*and when beholden they are nothing short but golden.*

*Like from the aura of the Mona Lisa…*
*from the glow of a snowflake in winter,*
*from the rapture of an instrument player*
*while performing in an orchestra,*
*they all relay messages that cannot be mistaken,*
*like feeling shaken from an earth emphatically quakened*
*using words that are notably*
*but sometimes audibly unspoken.*
*So, remember… verbalizing it is not the only way to crystalize it.*

## Why Perfection

*Teetering on the edge of time before re-entry*
*into the eternity of creation*
*oblivious of the folly found in self- annihilation*
*I stand transfixed as I analyse the mix*
*in the addiction of this attractive yet deceptive oblivion,*
*but on a whim, I trim my thoughts to the brim…*
*clean and slim*
*and without hesitation took a test on my intuition*
*gleaning from the answers to the question*
*about the spills and thrills accrued in the quest*
*for your illusive perfection.*

*A rousing angelic round of applause immediately enveloped*
*as he pronounced the myriad of things*
*that out of nothing could develop.*
*How miracles of creation from humans can sprout*
*from thoughts beamed thru enlightened minds*
*transcribed into words and modulated*

*by an obedient, poetic mouth...*
*carved by hands and fingers dangling about*
*from our sides... loosely and dangerously hanging out.*

*"Creation children, be wary just the same...*
*for the destruction of imperfection will not wane*
*it lurks for the perks and is always ready to pounce*
*to do battle for every inch to consume every ounce.*

*My children... victory for earth's reality*
*is certainly not a cinch*
*but the rewards of my perfection*
*is definitely within the pinch*
*It's waiting for the ones burning with desire*
*To reach up into the skies... to go higher and higher*

*Perfection my children, is within your grasps...*
*to touch... to clinch*
*But please, don't give up... stay focus, no hocus pocus...*
*please, don't flinch."*

# A Floral Cathedral
## Part 1

Welcome my friends... why yes, you can enter...

but please be tender

And with good behaviour apparent

you must almost be reverent

As you meander between those pious pews

of porous petals... precious

As if arranged by hands celestial

those front yard flower gardens... in actual

Were compartments of a botanical cathedral

that among other things

connected the visual to the floral.


Oh yes, my friends... that Pelican street of cathedrals

had overlords within

And we believe it is a sin

not to document the lifestyles and doctrine

**Illustration by Waheeda Ramnath**

*Of deceased Gilkes, Cardinez, Edwards,*
*Morgan and Nen Pantin*
*and on 83 not out from Cicada*
*we celebrate the pleasant, "quick-witted"*
*affable Ms. Cynthia...*
*who it is blatant... will be another*
*"well done my good and faithful servant"*

*and on Matapal we have a centurion*
*and still batting...*
*the unflappable, unshakeable Mrs. Evelyn...*
*their wisdom and tough love discipline,*
*and how they totally neglected obscenity,*
*rejected the "cuss-out your neighbour" mentality,*
*and instead preferred to be always cordial...*
*especially the Browns,*
*Ms. Rita, Ms. Zilma, Ms. Cynthia*
*and not just occasional but perennial...*
*always jovial they kept the Pelican / Cicada junction*
*full of lyrics... full of gumption*

*for example, they could transform a normal wayfarer*
*into a formal, well educated*
*full blown floral connoisseur*
*and an atmosphere violent into one heavenly*
*and the human animal element*
*into one adorned with civility,*
*one spiritually resilient.*

*And as you go from yard to yard*
*devoid of anything genuinely sad*
*All perimeter wall-less and pitbull-less*
*for easy access...*
*there you became enveloped in the rapture of flora*
*and fauna... sights and sound*
*With full orchestration in the sanctuary*
*of those flower gardens*
*where classical high notes of creation abound*
*Where colours, shapes and perfumes of heaven*
*are encoded and stored in sacks of pollen*
*That squirt out the nozzle*

*beyond chlorophylled leaves that rustle
round their maternal stems.
And out there, almost in mid-air,
it erupts into a flower pursued by a choir
of well-rehearsed fauna*

*spearheaded by the reversible whistling winged
hovering humming birds and buzzing bees
sounding like African drumming
and with grace and beauty you cannot muzzle
those wing bedecked floating butterflies
that go air borne to dazzle
with ramajay, chirp, skirt and flirt
in search of our neighbourhood's serenity*

*In harmony with that symphony
of cosmic floral tapestry....
those female custodians,
those heavenly creations....swaying majestically, sparkling
like crown jewellery...*

*those diadems, those sweet sensations*

*embedded with natural nectar concoctions*

*and other unknown medicinal gems*

*that sometimes randomly sprout, plum and bloom*

*straight out of the dirt*

*My friends it is a cert…*

*that in those cathedrals you could enter,*

*worship, wade, wink and wonder.*

# A Floral Cathedral
## Part 2

*In those cathedrals... a collage of signals*

*converge on an innocent convert's senses*

*As you behold the heavenly treasure*

*unfurled in floral sculpture*

*carved by the poetic words that rolled off the tongue*

*of an obviously artistic creator.*


*And as you stand amazed*

*within the overlords' gaze...*

*their faces beaming irresistible smiles, styles and skills*

*strategically emanating from varnished window shills*

*All the time... reflecting the thrills*

*generated from the waltz and rhyme*

*of their Dancing Daffodils,*

*flaming poinsettias, helliconias,*

*daisies mixed with dahlias*

*and you can almost hear anthems crescendoed*

*by chrysanthemums in chorus with anthuriums*
*about those proud old maids for certain*
*not intimidated by encroaching colour clad crotons*

*All tempting you to display poses*
*right in front their delicate roses*
*But beware over there... where they order the Ixora*
*to be put right next to the Queen of Flower*

*below drooping orchids hanging from rooftops*
*with flares not dissimilar to crystal chandeliers*
*emitting filtered light rays, rained...like those*
*strained thru stained window panes...*
*applauding God's laws right outside our doors,*
*the same that cause starry nights*
*and those blissful sunny days.*

*In our cathedral there was no blunder*
*and the chimes of those sublime times*
*still resonates asunder.*

*Yes, I still hear those chimes, I still see those climbs*

*up towering palm trees, bougainvillea,*

*Hibiscus like sentinels in the breeze…*

*camouflaging those candle-flies flashing,*

*crickets lurching with ants*

*marching across branches arching, vines spiraling …*

*all stealthily steepling towards the sky, yet...*

*rooted because of their toil in the fertile riverbank soil*

*A twinkling memory of a street called Pelican*

*in a region stigma-less and radiant*

*for the things you saw and heard were not just good*

*but a country mile beyond excellent…*


*and I vividly remember you know…*

*peeling thru my Blaupunt*

*and the neighbours' Redifussion Radio "*

*" the Roses of the South" concerto,*

*played by Ebonites Steel orchestra,*

*melodic and therapeutically slow*

*with a mellow baseline echo below,*

'Twas a symphony of community pan players…

spontaneous and to us very famous

And there was top down angelic musical influence all around

especially when the skillful Gwenny Browne

with cuatro and the S.D.A Movalites

took to gospel song


and on Sundays, the aroma from maternal cooking

ascended with exotic flavour

when mixed with the tonal twang

of Mr. Cournand's Hawaiian guitar.


And one and all was proud to grow

exposed to the glow

of those floral Cathedrals

built with a Moral, high on a Pedestal

… and even today when by Timo on Cicada you go,

you'll find a relic of Leotaud's floral Cathedral

perched on a plateau

and as you ascend towards its moorings

*amongst glittering stardust around you*

*cylindrically soaring… and with just that glimpse,*

*you will feel the jewel revealed from beneath terrain*

*mountainous… its beauty concealed*

*and to us it remains stigma-less and blest,*

*resplendent and resilient, forever filled…*

*with bouquets of memories Bridal but bombarded*

*with wreaths for the untimely, unnatural funeral*

*This unworded floral Cathedral is kept alive*

*in the heart of our beloved…*

*different almost succulent,*

*clinical almost super-natural,*

*vibrant always verdant, ummm…*

*it sweet, this riveting stimulant … Morvant.*

*I love you… and~ thank you Ms. Cynthia*

*for being a big part of my fond memories*

*and thank you all for same. ~*

*to have walked through those portals is my fame*

# A Shady Immortelle

When one is called into Planet Earth's testing arena
You don't know what or who you will meet
So God used deceased Milton and Leotha
To gift us Util… a daughter, friend, sister,
aunty, granny, a wife, a mother

Mixed with ingredients… soothing and sweet.
And according to her son Frankos
When she was in the pink
To highlight the memorable things about her
You did not have to stutter…
you did not have to think .

You will never find a more genuine person
That never choose to pretend
You always knew exactly what she stood for
Before you hit the curve in an approaching bend.

Util Auldress Henry.
13/2/1934 - 17/10/2012
"An evergreen memory of a sibling... blown across the blue."

*And if you wanted a warrior*
*to fight in your corner... until the bitter end*
*Util's strength and unwavering courage was guaranteed...*
*it was not a fleeting trend.*

*And so I write this poem...*
*a fitting tribute about her life to give*
*Mere words strain to explain*
*the heights she did attain*
*With the seventy-eight plus years on earth*
*that she had a chance to live.*

*From Tobago to Pelican, Pashley and villages deep south*
*in Siparia and Chirkoo*
*Going with their kids*
*where ever Telly had to hit the pavement*
*With his Adventist, Frontier style, stone crushing...*
*culporter and teacher shoe.*
*Util and her clan never turned back*

*It was up the rocky road with them she went*
*Leaving us cool memories with lengthening shadows*
*Cast from the brilliant life on earth she spent.*


*She flew to Brooklyn then Atlanta*
*with those long working hours to push thru*
*And before we knew...*
*God checked her into a lush valley in Heaven*
*To spontaneously enjoy a chuckle or two...*
*embellished with her signature joy and glee*
*Like the gentle breezes that rustle*
*thru the leaves of a shady immortelle tree.*

## Set On A Hill

When we first met… there was love and great joy
but there was no fret
when God decided to set
the Morvant S.D.A Church on this spot,
where wayfarers could find God's words divine
mixed with living water the thirsty to quench…
responding to things nitty gritty made sense,
So… to locate this Great Church
must facilitate, minimal search.

So he set it on a hill on the Pelican Street border
with "Africa", overlooking
the village main road…
from where souls, worth more than gold and silver,
could launder
as they watch the "Sunshine River" meander
around the grudgingly yet stubbornly
level playing field,

*teaming with potential for spiritual yield,*
*a brother's keeper with glittering sword and shield.*

*And so… its members got the commission*
*to build on this lot,*
*'twas from the foundation God carved out his purpose*
*on a pedestal of a plot*
*and if you do your research… 'twas from this church*
*his light he did perch*

*and for the next fifty plus years it did fill*
*this blest community with the wisdom of God's will*
*and with words to highlight the Signs of the Times*
*so the people could see and avoid*
*ramifications of crimes*
*as they Bob and Weave between testing lines*
*towards an horizon we all inevitably encroach…*
*wandering wayfarers incoherently approach*
*those voices with strategic sermons*
*radiating from the rostrum of this church.*

*And so… to you brave pilgrims all,*
*you ought to stand tall*
*as I give this tribute for the road that you tread.*
*You inspire with your fire, refine when you combine,*
*travail when good things must prevail,*
*the wicked and stone-hearted you beseech*
*the dysfunctional you teach,*
*the inflicted you soothe and restore hope into their weary*
*soul… you take a Good Samaritan stroll,*
*I see you clearly… the poor and hungry*
*you replenish regularly.*

*So this tribute that I give to you comes from the heart*
*and the head too*
*about your doctrine to quickly erase sin*
*combined with responding with speed*
*to the community need,*
*like with the multitude he did feed…*
*it is not just by your word, but more importantly,*
*it is by your deed… your kingdom work will succeed.*

*And to this church on the hill…*

*I bear no ill will, for as good neighbours go*

*you're way ahead of the flow,*

*you are an asset to our community*

*and I thank you sincerely*

*for your fifty plus years of neighbourhood presence*

*as the embodiment of Godly reverence*

*and I wish you continued growth*

*driven by Biblical substance.*

*Thank You Neighbour*

*For your labour of love generated from above*

*Thank you kindly*

## Listen To The Night

As the weary sun takes its final afternoon dip…
the creator gives the switch a flip and in a stitch…
the moon and stars appear to twinkle and twitch
and it's the right and plight of our sight
and a convoy of senses to take flight

but far away from the fading traffic hum, I realized…
my lagging ear drums continue to strum
and eventually succumb
to the well -organized almost synchronized;
jazzing almost haunting sounds of the night.

My friends… the things you hear
from the dark ignite a spark
that resonates thru your soul with a spirit so sweet
it climaxes at dawn when daylight switches on
and another night you salivate to meet,
and when it's finally here shadows comfort despair

when nocturnal melodies are composed everywhere
I'm always amazed at the sounds I hear
when I'm dazed and with the night
I'm totally phased.

Oh, its nightfall that's all… to trigger a hoot or a call
from the black box of an eagle's flight,
after a rugged descent
or is it a hawk relaxing triumphantly,
exercising its vocal chords with ominous frequency
after a predator's day soaring silently…
was well spent,
and before I expire I'm kept up by piercing cricket appeals
as if to a presiding umpire
in unison yet leapfrogging

a well-rehearsed croaking choir,
and I could attest, it's the interlude I love best…
tweeted by an entertaining migrating bird
taking a rest from its planetary quest

*to a beckoning almost magnetizing,*

*southern summer's nest.*


*And out of the dark another spark...*

*from a mate feeling great or is it a suitor that's late*

*or is he or she scared or angry*

*at the howl of a hunting coyote*

*that we could clearly hear but just cannot see...*


*and the familiar neighborhood rooster*

*with a gentle reminder*

*of Peter's epic self- preservation dilemma that night...*

*when he retreated undercover*

*to become an innocent by-stander*

*to the extreme trauma Jesus had to suffer,*

*makes me wonder*

*about the timing of the neighborhood rooster,*

*especially that night...*

*along a busily crowded and dirgefully shrouded*

*Via Dolorosa.*

Illustration by Waheeda Ramnath

*My friends, those sensations come*
*on the wings of a breeze*
*that rustle then rumble with lightning*
*flexing its muscle*
*and after that crescendo my senses follow*
*into tomorrow*

*the beat of drizzling raindrops*
*caressing galvanize rooftops,*
*soothing and mellow whispering in my ear...*
*my head swirling on my pillow,*

*and to me, those melodic dynamics*
*seemed to be the preamble of a classical dream*
*and when you interpret it...*
*you know that indeed, it's an out-of-sight theme.*
*Oh, yes my friends... those sounds from the dark*
*keep igniting a spark*
*that hasten a noisy day away with a lesson,*
*'bout the laugh of a lark*

*harmonizing in acapella*
*with a canine tenor coming in*
*with not just an ordinary bark*
*but an operatic arc weaving alto,*
*baritone and soprano...*
*sounding stupendously as if in an eco-symphony,*
*performing instinctively and in close proximity*
*to movement with poetry*
*of a rippling river running thru the center of our*
*virtuoso verdant, melody potent pulsating park...*
*can't you hear it...*

*it's just another moonlit, musical site*
*given so the human and all the other heavenly bodies orbiting*
*in the still of the night*
*in search of respite... finally here on earth*
*we could studiously listen*
*and our lives will no longer be*
*an empty, restless, dreamless plight*

*cause… we could totally relax*

*forgetting daytime facts*

*and soar from the ground floor thru the daytime door*

*like a windblown, un-mannered kite;*

*airborne …we could now delight*

*in the subtle melodies*

*that compose the music*

*of our dramatic, dreamy night.*

## Behind God's Back

Behind God's back... I find extremely brilliant
Even though I'm city transparent...
in search of an urban stimulant
with attributes inherent and side effects apparent,
I find those rural revelations strange
and sometimes surreal,
Except when, reluctantly or even inadvertently...
I snuggle up to nature and experience the rapture
its warm emotions I can feel.

It's the destination away from hectic traffic
devoid of static yet...
cluttered with ideas all flooded with universal appeal
where secrets belonging to heaven,
behind God's back... he can subliminally reveal.

Behind God's back you can hear rivers ripple
as they go cascading spontaneously composing refrains

*over blissful terrains…*

*about imposing hills protecting reposing dales*

*as village folks settle showing their mettle,*

*tending cattle and trimming sails.*

*Behind God's back wayfarers gravitate*

*To revive faded dreams imaginations collate*

*It's where animal instincts postulate*

*for spiritual passions that can make you levitate*

*over stressful people as you effortlessly meditate.*

*It's where the grey skies of the city stagnate*

*then mutate and pulsate*

*like a diamond that radiates*

*mind blowing astrological scenes*

*with their beams*

*the only neighbors that could afford*

*to live way beyond their means.*

*Behind God's back is where life's elements converge
with ecstasy as they merge
like in the spinal cord of a human
that receives just a semblance of a surge.*

*Behind God's back is where shadows gather
And devious people with nefarious intentions clamor
But have no fear God's word is anchored there
girded in resplendent armor*

*And remember… you can satisfy the lack
if you jump the track
and go full circle to behold an elusive miracle….
camouflaged in something simple
doing something resembling humble and subtle…
so don't abuse and senselessly hijack
don't rape the ecoscape with enterprising speed
and insatiable greed,
don't go on the attack.*

*that short-lived prosperity will escape us…*

*and as a whole we will not*

*victoriously achieve our goal,*

*because the lack of functionality and sustainability*

*of our life's high quality will return to haunt us*

*from the remotest part of his anatomy.*

*Please don't test his sensitivity, respiring in his lungs*

*and woven in other critical organs very intricately*

*Residing circumspectly and supernaturally…*

*out there where the air is rare,*

*there is enlightenment beyond compare…*

*somewhere behind God's back.*

## A Shakespearean Refrain

There was this moment of inspiration
while participating in a two-way conversation…
Filled with concern I listened to Elder Gemma talk
about preparing the children
for the mix of life's close encounters
filled with thrills
and its fair share of challenging dilemmas.

She beamed with Pride and great Admiration
when she referred to a student
that was able to highlight a Shakespeare quotation
while chatting in relaxation
after an intense Gemsville Music Class Session.

She said the quote reproduced by this literate student
spoke…"Of a man without music… as having no heart,"
and according to a bewildered Shakespeare …

**Artwork by Alice X.Zhang**

"A man with no music

denies all things joyous and holy…"

and Shakespeare said "I shall trust no such man."


This quote made me remember with good reason and no pain

another Shakespearean Refrain about…

"if music is the food of life we should play on,"


and as our conversation continued to soar

into the possibilities contained

in her music students' horizon,

we could see clearly that music

well written and executed

can usher you into the very presence of God…

its creator and Lord.


Music is a gift designed for those

that are not just barely living…

it's a spectacular reward.

*Music… can be used as a vehicle to take you places*
*good or bad, happy or sad*
*it striates or soothes… motivates or deflates…*
*stimulates or sedates…*
*it puts you in the mood*
*but it don't mean a thing if it ain't got a swing[1]*
*and the lyrics, melody and harmony*
*can't activate the holy spirit*
*implanted deep within.*

*You can either apply its pros or its cons,*
*decide if you want to push your listeners apart*
*or let them be drawn together*
*in spontaneous bonds.*

*You have a choice…*
*your music deserves a good message,*
*instrument and or voice.*
*Music is one of God's basic developmental tools*
*that a child could take thru the days of his/her life*

*it helps that child appreciate*
*and be part of a universal language*
*filled with creativity and with God's inspiration rife.*

*And it follows that one day into being a composer*
*you may find your way*
*and although it may not be in music*
*that your skills will have sway*
*the discipline of practice to make perfect...*
*will definitely come into play*

*And agreeing with Shakespeare, who many years ago*
*composed a luscious and precious refrain that is profound*
*yet simple and plain and it is*
*" Ummm...Music is the food of life..." my children.*
*So Right On, Maestro... You budding Virtuoso,*
*"Play On..." as you pick up the mantle*
*"Play on...*
*" you are the lighted wick in God's candle,*
*"Play on..." as you grow*

*"Play on… "*

*and let the river of well - modulated musical sound abound as it continues to flow.*

## The Flair Of The Floating Violin

With all systems successfully deployed

we were buoyed by the joy of our brand new toy

and with full throttle unleashed ...

America was within our reach

and like a stallion we were riding the waves

with authority when suddenly...

and it was not a drill, human error

nor any other strategic decoy

but definitely it was a genuine ICEBERG AHOY...

ICEBERG AHOY... ICEBERG AHOY

Radio Soundblaster from a traumatized broadcaster

and although the impending impact

was not just seismic but astronomic

yet, I was deeply moved, totally consumed

even mortally distracted

by the most spirited, emphatic, enigmatic

LIVE music performance

ever staged on this planet.

*And as the captain of this liner / eternal Titanic*

*observer cum poetic narrator*

*I advise you to attach your life jacket*

*to the back of your mind*

*and if you have time walk with a warm blanket*

*and the impressions of his searching violin's strings of velvet*

*Cause… his curtain call came*

*in the midst of an awesome, unforgiving and oh yes…*

*avaricious ebb and flow*

*under a starry,*

*surrounded by an understandably chaotic,*

*well chilled unapologetic, misty atmospheric*

*silhouetted glow,*

*but his… his was a rare demo*

*of a professional musician's intricate*

*and very warm human show*

*where he played on with flair*

*using unparalleled romantic gear*

*oozing with musical eloquence*

*overflowing with more than sufficient spiritual substance.*

*Oh yes, it ain't no jest… he and his band played on with flair*
*away from the glare,*
*aware that there were no lifeboats left…*
*their lives to safety will steer;*

*and when his time to meet his maker drew near,*
*this bandmaster instinctively strapped his violin,*
*like his curvaceous sweetheart baby, around his body;*
*and as the sand in his time glass emptied slow*
*I believe it was without fear, regret or sorrow;*
*that…well bedecked, I could see clearly,*
*this wounded player methodically jumped…*
*from the skywardly tilting deck*
*into the swirling graveyard*
*patiently awaiting below.*

*Oh Hartley, the people of this Planet*
*and not just your fiancée Maria*

*salute, adore and admire your dedication*

*and dramatic rapid fire…*

*which were simply introductory to your ultimate bravery.*


*And I believe… it was within a biblical scale*

*like Jonah preserved in the belly of a whale*

*that some ten days after the sinking of the Titanic*

*the strapped violin was retrieved*

*from Hartley's dead body*

*…………floating in the Atlantic.*


*It was returned to Maria, the original gift giver,*

*then… with a shining metallic reminder highlighting the*

*loving sentiment of its tender sweetheart sender.*


*But now, this specially chosen rosewood violin*

*was transformed into something*

*of an organic heart mender*

*silently and almost surgically*

*healing the broken heart of his lifelong spinster*

*left dangling from the static of a lost*
*entangling with a soulmate who in crisis*
*rendered service when he gave all he had…*
*that timely, crucial, gospel music.*

*'Twas a task…done in conditions*
*conducive to unmask his rare human spirit and logic …*
*which to me, was nothing short of being*
*functionally angelic.*

*Then… many years after in 2006,*
*it was resoundingly characteristic*
*to see this violin float again in the dusty chamber*
*an amateur musician's attic.*

*Then, recently in 2013…*
*precisely a century after that historic, inaugural infamous,*
*catastrophic journey*
*it was both ironic and poetic when it floated $1.6m (USD)*
*in an auctioneer's market*
*'twas a record breaking Titanic artifact*
*sale of an item deemed both authentic and heroic.*

*And now, today…anywhere you go you can grow*
*just gazing at this buffeted instrument's photo*
*as you follow lessons lurking in shadow*
*dancing to the crescendo*
*of the ship's haunting horn blow,*
*enjoying no sweeter music you can imagine*
*emanating from this muted musician's compelling*

*and oh yes… soggy, unplayable violin*
*meditatively resting in his*
*varnished leather casing nursing comatose strings*
*continuously reverberating*
*a voice-less echo in concert*
*with his conspicuously missing, leather case breaching,*
*ship-wreck repelling*
*and eventually load shedding… strumming bow.*


*And I believe, it was released*
*with tears of a fiddler's flow*
*when the bow Hartley had to reluctantly…let go.*


*But… Thank you, Wallace Hartley*
*for reminding us of the things*
*that only the solace of finding God's destiny know,*
*as we wrap our minds around the self-less things*
*that night… that you did,*
*things that only a solid spiritual foundation*
*would support from beneath your unassuming*

*and oh yes… specially anointed lid.*

*Because… 'twas on top of the trauma
I know you had to suffer…
makes me always ponder the wonder
and admire your valor when, that night,
you decided it was your duty to deliver
the utility of a town-crier.*

*That Night… when to soothe a common plight
you and your band made a one of a kind stand
when you played on stoically…
with both musical and spiritual overtures
processed miraculously
between the rush
of your unraveling audience's frenetic mind,*

*with the nights' dynamics recorded meticulously
between the gusts of the ship's gasping,
operatically howling*

*and to my chagrin resolution-less and absolution-less*

*sympathetic wind…*

*and in the reality of non-negotiability…*

*and at the mercy of the situation's irreversibility,*

*below a watchful skyglow,*

*alert with your teary-eyed gusto*

*adrenalised by those flares…*

*that stream of screaming, airborne lighted arrows*

*that crystallised a horizon already marginalized…*

*because of those unanswered*

*gradually dimming distress halos,*

*yet to you… already sermonized, 'twas a priority…*

*in the wake of the encroaching fury*

*of a watery Grand Finale*

*to motion your band, to play at least one last ditty*

*to steady the fluttering hearts of a fragile humanity*

*and I knew that to you it was not too late to postulate*

*with an appropriate simulated concerto*

*with movements to facilitate*

*the approaching gate not…*
*with a discordant audio predicament*
*but a joyous spontaneous symphonic stereo sentiment*
*that resonates thru the pages of the ages*
*above those seismic vibrations*
*liberal with dysfunctions, blindfolded and surreal*
*but for your reactions that night*
*its terror and paralyzing trepidations*
*were transformed into a powerful, soul stirring, perennial appeal…*
*when swiftly you and your band modulated*
*the melody "Nearer My God to Thee"*
*to underpin the need for those scurrying seafarers*
*and the increasing numbers*
*of daily hell bound oblivious,*
*distracted sojourners*
*to searchingly repent their sins.*
*Oh yes my friends, that night*
*Hartley harnessed a cosmiculous conversation opportunity*
*when unwaveringly and quick to discern*

*he embraced a task*

*ordinary earthlings would not conceive*

*or even be concerned,*

*but clearly this Samaritan musician*

*with a heart of gold*

*would pay dearly to be his brother's keeper,*

*and to me this music lover*

*was more than just a compulsive serenader*

*who surrendered himself into the role*

*of the sinking Titanic's sacrificial town-crier,*

*but most importantly, he was a reliant*

*soul worthy navigator.*

*And oh… what a musical twist*

*with the metamorphosis*

*of this entertainer instrumentalist*

*into an anthem-playing, altar-calling,*

*destiny changing evangelist.*

*And even though he was totally petrified yet defiant…*
*he played on;*
*devastated yet steadfast… he played on*
*and when the die was cast, on deck…*
*he and his band were among the last.*

*He played on until the bitter end, my friend.*
*And although, that night …the natural battle*
*he did not win,*
*yet… that floating violin interlude*
*made me conclude that he was akin*
*with the Northern Star compass spin*
*he played on and not even the surging ocean*
*compounded by man's gloating imperfection,*
*that effort… his assumed duty…*
*God's purpose and destiny even in calamity…*
*his resolve those elements could not dissolve*
*those elements that night could not… rescind.*
*So Thank You, Wallace Hartley…*
*wherever you may be,*

*and for all we know, probably reclining in heaven*

*after a riveting musical show*

*Thank you Hartley… Thank you and your band, Sincerely.*

**Wallace Hartley**

P.S… Rest in Peace, my brother Hartley.
The poetry and theology of your way

*have composed a classical life story of your day*
*and it makes me sway*
*to that windy, mellifluous, onshore Atlantic melody*
*that keeps gently reminding me*
*that those breezy notes of your anxiously*
*unfinished doxology, rendered with this…*
*this floating violin harmoniously*
*complying with your band's mellow music making*
*methodology,*
*have not been lost inadvertently nor irretrievably*
*at sea.*

*And finally Hartley, the plot of your sunspot revealed*
*between the silhouette of your sunrise and sunset*
*is still radiating a ray of ultra- selfless signals today.*

*So thank you very much for your musical touch*
*and thank you very kindly*
*for the anxiety insularity*
*provided by your blissful symphony.*

*And from the lips of this unflinching captain*

*on the bridge of my skywardly tilting ship…*

*I say you deserve*

*a reward with a heavenly tip*

*with which to thank you Hartley*

*thank you and your band sincerely.*

*And with cosmic accord, Hartley…you put on record*

*a performance that was like the swell or flare*

*of a wave or flame…*

*because no other recital on this planet would ever surf*
*the atmosphere quite the same.*

*So see you around, Hartley...*
*when the Titanic's memory will again produce poetry*
*and live symphonies will recapture*
*the luster and glitter*
*of the musical festivities that prevailed*
*on board my ocean strider,*
*before that encounter*
*with the uninvited party pooper.*

*So see you later and I know it will be greater*
*on the other side of this merciless ocean's*
*bottomless, shadow-less, music-less plunder*
*and I am only going under to put asunder*
*that inexcusable blunder*
*that muted the floating rhythms of my musical liner.*
*And I say, to my crew and every passenger...*
*"at my order, we will again go cruising*

*over yonder and just remember,*

*my word… is my eternal binder."*

# *A Most Beautiful Day!*

*As I traverse this treacherous terrain of life*

*fused with cliffs and unexpected ifs*

*and littered along the way*

*with precarious rocks that sway*

*over valleys strewn with strife*

*interspersed with ridges rife with grooves…*

*grooves that cut like a knife*

*and to my dismay…*

*those images blur the vision*

*of what is a most, a most beautiful day.*


*And along this road*

*on which this marathon race is run,*

*beware because it is laced with relics*

*and vestiges of illusive promises*

*and relays of deceptive mirages*

*that dance with attitude consumed*

*with human latitude*

*coming at you with pace*

*as if shot from the nozzle of a gun.*


*And as I go and grow into this enthralling sky show...*

*I got to know that the moon, stars and sun*

*were set as beacons since...*

*since time had begun,*


*oh yes my friends those simmering, shimmering, flickering*

*flames stay burning in space with grace*

*and without pay hanging around patiently*

*and silently... orbiting in functional proximity*

*to feed and delight our day*

*and on earth... we were created erect,*

*jotting straight out of the dirt*

**Hubble Telescope Image**

*and just like the trees*
*we ought to intentionally modulate*
*the breeze  blowing praises*
*to the one weaving that universal bond;*
*criss-crossing creeds leap frogging galaxies*
*with intrinsic similarities resembling love…*
*constantly beaming from up above.*

*Oh yes my friends, those heavenly bodies*
*play cyclical games*
*before reluctantly shedding their glory,*
*sometimes eclipsed…*
*behind shadow soaked shrouds*
*and other windblown clouds*
*that tell a dark compelling story.*

*Oh yes… those drunken strays*
*can cause spasmodic yet spectacular delays*
*and to God's credit*
*it's according to how you see it…*

*so just be accurate*

*when you evaluate his treasure trove*

*of sparkling diamonds radiating positive opinions,*

*for when you navigate*

*using fear and negativity as the priority*

*it increases your susceptibility*

*to a clandestine and most importantly…*

*a depressed mentality,*

*to complete this race*

*you must let purity and integrity set the pace*

*towards sustainability and incrementally…*

*spiritual clarity.*


*This Quest… this horizon…*

*this, this beaming yet buffeting sea*

*could be like a prison from which your destiny*

*strives to let you go free*

*and over there via the strength of your will*

*you'll find tools for your goal…*

*respite for your spirit, rewards for your soul.*

Oh, what a day.... terminal at worst, eternal at best
and to quench the thirst and rebuke the curse
it's replete with your love
and filled with your word... to withstand the test.


And as I scan his necklace of orbiting gems
he has in your array,
I stand here on earth today and say
that it may be treacherous
but at least it's spontaneous...
and I like the challenge anyway.


Search the cosmos and you won't see
a better multiplication of a ray
complete with amplification of the splendor
to achieve attenuation of the rancor
in this universal arena...
it's like a needle in a stack of hay.


So be wise, open your eyes...

*it's an idea generating franchise*

*but the Roaring Lion is not here to play.*

*Just think about it, and you will see*

*that inspite of, notwithstanding and or nevertheless...*

*we are blest, cause we are located but not duplicated*

*in a most... a most beautiful day.*

## A Gentle Reminder

"What did you do?"

whispered the voice with the musical tune

"about the Rosebud I gave you…

to sprout and to prune,

Did you do like the wise virgins

as time stealthily scurried along?

Did you prepare for life's special occasion …?

did you practice the notes of a classical song?"

The voice was gentle …

it peeled over a musical whistle

about the tasks heaven contented

for which I was responsible.

He said, "I came back this morning

thru the pouring rain… to the cusp

of a dawning again.

*to adjust the miniscule things*
*about which you complain*
*to see if you are taking the pain*
*and if you from procrastination abstain*
*and, most importantly, to hear you explain*
*the reasons the rosebud will achieve full gain."*

*This close encounter had some well-mannered static*
*for success is not automatic*
*in heaven and earth, strategies must be implemented*
*for good habits to be cemented.*

*In times of disappointment or fear… a word,*
*a glance or as much as an appropriate slight touch*
*could transform the potential*
*of an unassuming looking rosebud*
*into a spectacular flare.*

*My friends, the joys of parenting may be few,*
*but remember, rich rewards are guaranteed you*

with biblical implications, citations
or even a poetic recitation
your life on earth has a heavenly dimension.

And when life's wind chill factor blows cold...
cuddle your kiddo and stay warm in the soul
be a good role model and God will bless you
and your household on the double,
and like the virgins wise
that prepared for the groom...
"the rosebud I gave you will sprout, plum and flare
into a magnificent bloom."

My friends, the verses of this poem
are a gentle reminder to you
that there is no more important task given to two
than the responsibilities related to care and nurture...
but beware
for when one of the two turns out to be a spoiler
or a deserter

*the reward for the other turns out to be even greater.*
*"So, stay strong my friends and I will be with you*
*all functional couples and single parents too*
*Stay strong, as I churn up mysteries*
*for you to discern.*

*Stay strong... and we will have another*
*two-way face to face conversation on my return*
*to the cusp of a brand new dawn embedded*
*in another unassuming looking morn.*
*Stay strong, you subtle mindscaper...*
*stay strong, you personality shaper,*
*this is just another gentle reminder, stay strong."*

# It's Already Been Done

"It's already been done!" I heard a voice say
As I paused between plans
that refused to obey my commands.
"It's been done... long before you prepared the essay
you now write with arrogance and gumption... today! "


And as I continued my trek...
the voice gently beckoned and checked
my direction along the road,
it perused my imagination at times...
rearranged contours and signs
As I fumbled with the compass I use to plot my goal
"The story of life has already been told,
it's already been done... packaged and sold."


"It's been done..." came another whisper
forcing me to ponder
calamities inherent in an approaching blind corner,

*Then I heard, "don't panic about things strategic,*
*it's not just optic*
*cause... from the foundation I sequenced events*
*in the right place,*
*Your skills I don't condemn but...*
*I calmed the storm in the midst of mayhem*
*It is from my love that all your successes stem,*
*So beware of pride as you never have to save face...*
*reflect light as you walk in my grace*
*It's already been done, my son....*
*I have already won."*

*"It's been done..." soon grew into a tiff*
*cause all you see is a bluff*
*when I'm approaching a cliff,*
*beam of a star we take light years to see*
*is not just a glow but a twinkling illusion to me,*
*sites of a mirage that disappear in a figment*
*you capture with glee and deliver without payment*
*and use the mist of dark clouds*

*to colour the arch of a rainbow show*
*as you lessen the water flow*
*I hear you whisper…*
*"It's already been done, you know."*


*The voice I hear is soothing yet soul searching*
*with projections far-reaching without usurping*
*the options in current affairs… I could choose*
*It prompts but is not beseeching…*
*it allows but is not alluring*
*It jockeys without altering*
*the ramifications of today's news*
*it's already been done… way back in the pews,*
*It's as if my footsteps*
*have been described in your shoes*


*It's already been done… got no time for the blues*
*It's already been done…*
*vision is not restricted to hues*
*It's already been done…*

*to you I give the clue of clues*
*The voice said… "you need great faith…*
*when you are paying your dues.*

*Then… don't be surprise if at sunrise*
*there is a ten-fold refund,*
*Good or bad, happy or sad… you plant the seed*
*and I will grow it with speed*
*The war has already been won…*
*In my time…. it has already been done."*

# Patmos Rhapsody

Come... write these things you must
Well, that's why I brought you to Patmos
And without delay... to those churches please convey
These crucial things I say
" I am the Alpha and Omega...
the First and the Last,"
Brother John, Listen...
then, you gotta go write this letter
For my words will come to pass.

After the settling of the dust
I view the truth of Ephesus...
a church all evil things despise
I see it clearly with my eyes
I look again a little later and see a "First Love"
You can't remember.
"Oh, people can't you see...
a bit of Ephesus in you and me."

*And those who from poverty and tribulations suffer*
*Who are faithful and humble in the church of Smyrna*
*I hear your cry and do record your strife*
*And will reward you with a "Crown of Life."*
*"Oh, people can't you see…*
*a bit of Smyrna in you and me."*
*And to the slack be quick and count the cost*
*Your days are numbered in Thyatira and Pergamos.*

*You know the truth but you just won't bother*
*You harbor doctrines written by the other author.*

*I see idolatry, blasphemy, fornication and adultery…*
*among you today,*
*The ultimate price you will have to pay.*
*"Oh, people can't you see…*
*a bit of these folks in you and me."*

*Please tell this…*
*to the churches of Laodicea and Sardis,*

Your sum total have all gone amiss.


You poison the truth, you rot from the root
You are lukewarm and ready to die
Repent… for my judgement is nigh.


"Oh, people can't you see.
we need repentance in you and me."
Philadelphia's crescendo of love
We fit like a hand in a glove
An open door policy… no man can harm thee.


Philadelphia you'll inherit a song,
the heavenly host will all sing along
In perfect harmony, Jesu' love in you and me.


Patmos Rhapsody… a celestial melody
Love letters from the Son of Man.
Patmos Rhapsody… an inspired strategy
That tells us "it's time to make a stand."

*Oh, melody with sweet refrain,*

*Oh, melody with life to gain.*

*Patmos Rhapsody takes you to an eternal destiny*

*Serenaded by a heavenly symphony.*

*Amen.... Amen... Amen.*

**John-On The Isle Of Patmos**

# AN OPEN INVITATION

This poet thinks that inspirational poetry is an efficient yet under-utilized methodology that can be used to get "time-tested" Biblical truths to the people in a way they could understand and be enlightened for the rest of their days. At the same time inspirational poetry can uplift and relax the listener with thought provoking, wholesome entertainment. By and large inspirational poetry crystalizes profound messages needed in a world bombarded with negativity... because of this, I think that psalmists or troubadours should be quickly raised up to storm the kingdom of darkness with the light of God's words.

Toward this end, I would like to introduce you to "Sprouting Inspirational Poetry" (SIP). SIP provides potency in Spirituality and Civility. SIP can be used to motivate well-fed sleeping giants to wake-up and do something effective by simply digging up God-given talents buried in their lives. To get a SIP call me at 868-747-4141 and together we can customize an event or events to fit the need of your church, company or community group.

Think about it... the Shepherd, CEO or Team Captain can't do it alone and every song or profound message starts with a semblance of poetry which sharpens your vision and anyway a bit of inspirational poetry always augers well.

SIP has the potential to rekindle what Adam enjoyed while conversing with God in the cool of the evening. So join me in the proliferation of problem-solving inspired conversation instead of blindfolded, ear-plugged, self-serving one-way verbal tirades waging mayhem in the omega of our days. Let's take a SIP.

Contact me by email at poetrymorgan@gmail.com
or by Cell phone at
868-747-4141

**P.S....** If Christopher Columbus did not push his boat off its moorings on that morning... the New World would have dusted and rusted in the dock of that bay. So from way over there in your neck of the woods....

Let's take a SIP and raise the communication bar. The God of the Universe will smile and the Human Plight will take flight.... Enjoy.

# ABOUT THE POET

I was employed in the Government's Teaching Service before migrating to Canada and after returning to Trinidad in the 1977, I worked in a variety of environments from on air Broadcasting with 610 Radio, Computer Programming at the highest level, Computer Literacy and Programming Lecturer to Telecommunications Technician before pursuing a family health food manufacturing business with my wife.

On hindsight, I think the clutch of human activities that I was involved in, allowed me a cross-sectional view of society which, eventually, nourished my appetite for communication. In the final analysis, who am I to limit God's wisdom and reduce the impact of his clandestine tenacity in the shaping of my horizon even while my vision was blurred. God is good and his "I am" is my only tool in my quest to unwrap the sweetness of poetry... the language of angels.

# EDUCATION

Diploma in Computer Programming and Operations from Seneca College, Toronto Canada.

National Certificate in Domestic Electronics and Servicing Techniques from Ministry of Education, Trinidad and Tobago.

Uncertified course in Mass Media and Principles of Broadcasting from National Institute of Broadcasting, Toronto Canada.

## References
[1]Ellington, Duke. *It Don't Mean A Thing*. Comp. Duke Ellington. 1943.

www.ingramcontent.com/pod-product-compliance
Lightning Source LLC
Chambersburg PA
CBHW050553300426
44112CB00013B/1900